D0821802

WITHDRAWN

WOODLAND FOREST ECOSYSTEMS

by Racquel Foran

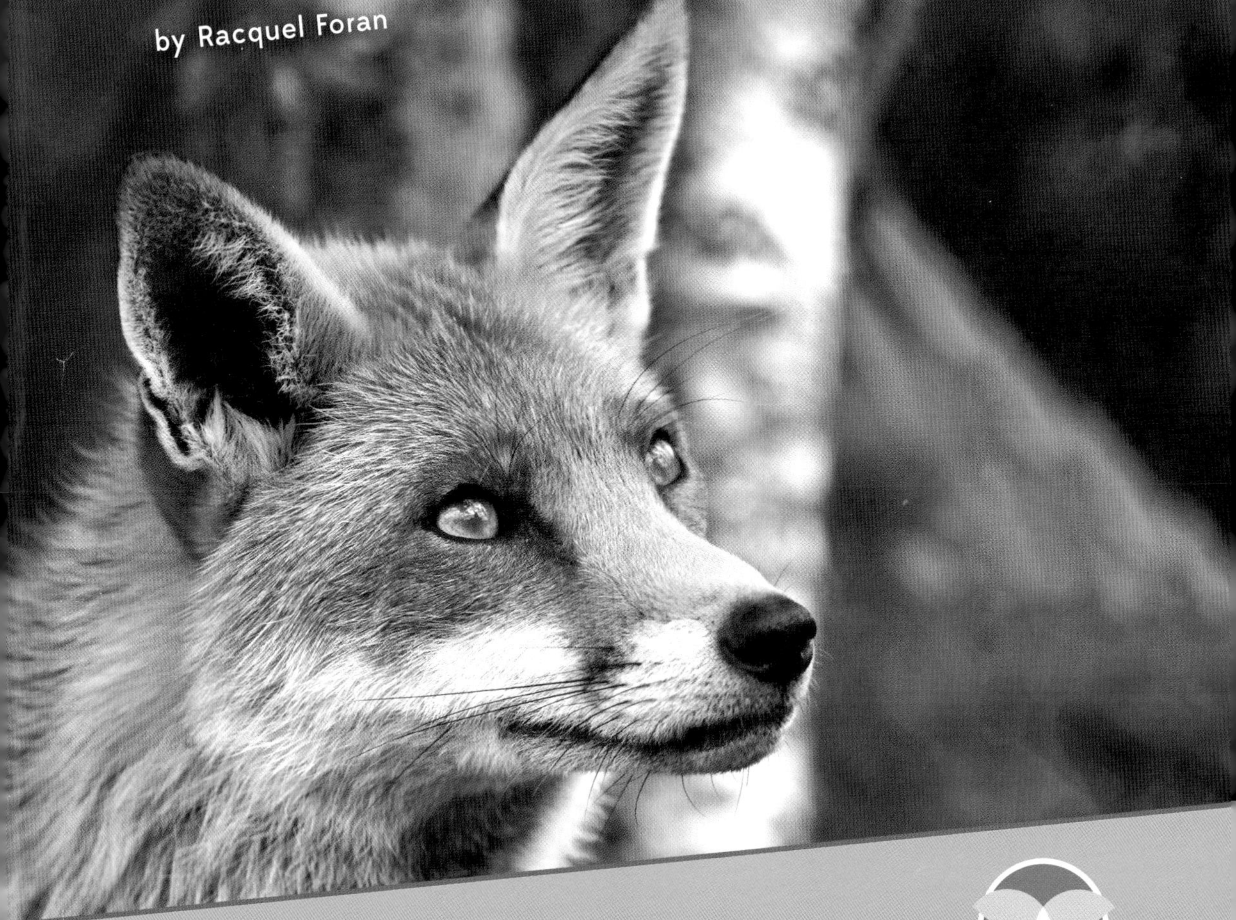

Content Consultant
David Greene
Professor, Forestry and Wildland Resources
Humboldt State University

Core Library

An Imprint of Abdo Publishing
abdopublishing.com

abdopublishing.com

Published by Abdo Publishing, a division of ABDO, PO Box 398166, Minneapolis, Minnesota 55439. Copyright © 2016 by Abdo Consulting Group, Inc. International copyrights reserved in all countries. No part of this book may be reproduced in any form without written permission from the publisher. Core Library™ is a trademark and logo of Abdo Publishing.

Printed in the United States of America, North Mankato, Minnesota
042015
092015

THIS BOOK CONTAINS
RECYCLED MATERIALS

Cover Photo: iStockphoto
Interior Photos: iStockphoto, 1, 4, 6, 8, 10, 14, 16, 18, 20, 28 (middle right), 28 (top right), 28 (middle left), 28 (bottom right), 32, 45; Design Pics/Yves Marcoux/Newscom, 12; Fredrik Norrsell/Danita Delimont Photography/Newscom, 22; Steve Brigman/Shutterstock Images, 24; Joe McDonald/Corbis, 27; Shutterstock Images, 28 (top left), 34; Jim Kruger/iStockphoto, 28 (bottom left); Neil Hardwick/Shutterstock Images, 28 (upper middle); Mihail Zhukov/iStockphoto, 28 (middle); Nathan Denette/The Canadian Press/AP Images, 38; Daisy Gilardini/Newscom, 43

Editor: Jon Westmark
Series Designer: Becky Daum

Library of Congress Control Number: 2015931584

Cataloging-in-Publication Data
Foran, Racquel.
 Woodland forest ecosystems / Racquel Foran.
   p. cm. -- (Ecosystems of the world)
Includes bibliographical references and index.
ISBN 978-1-62403-859-4
1. Forest ecology--Juvenile literature.   2. Forests--Juvenile literature.
I. Title.
577.3097--dc23

2015931584

CONTENTS

CHAPTER ONE

LIFE IN A WOODLAND FOREST

A 500-pound (227-kg) brown bear lumbers through the woods. It is in search of a big spring meal. It is late May. The bear is trying to gain weight it lost during hibernation, which ended in April. The hungry animal knows exactly where to go to fill its stomach.

The nearby river is packed with salmon. They are coming back from the ocean to reproduce. The fish

Brown bears may weigh twice as much before hibernation as they do in spring.

Coastal brown bears feed on salmon swimming up
freshwater streams to lay their eggs.

jump out of the water as they move upstream. The
bear wades into the water and swipes up a fish. First it
eats the fish's head, its favorite part. Then it swallows
the rest. After catching more than 20 fish, the bear
bites the head off of one final fish and tosses the
carcass toward shore. Satisfied, the big animal heads
back into the trees.

A crow swoops down and pecks at the salmon
remains. After the crow has eaten its fill, the fish's
remaining nutrients will seep into the soil for plants
to use.

Where in the World?

Forests cover approximately 30 percent of Earth. Trees are the main feature in all forests. But there are dozens of types of forests around the world. Each falls into one of three categories: boreal, temperate, or tropical. Boreal and temperate forests are also known as woodland forests. Brown bears live in woodland forests.

Boreal forests account for approximately 30 percent of Earth's forests. Marshes, rivers, lakes, and wetlands are common in the boreal. These forests span across

Salmon: Food and Fertilizer

Salmon play an important role in some forest ecosystems. They are the most important food source for coastal brown bears. Salmon also are a great source of fertilizer. Nearly all salmon die after laying their eggs. Plants near the water take up nutrients from the dead fish. These nutrients provide building blocks for healthy plants. Brown bears and birds also carry thousands of pounds of salmon into the forest. This allows plants far from rivers and streams to benefit from the nutrients that come from dead salmon.

The boreal forest is the world's largest land-based ecosystem.

Alaska, Canada, Scandinavia, and Russia. They cover 6.4 million square miles (16.6 million sq km).

Temperate forests are mainly found between boreal forests in the North and tropical regions near the equator. The temperature is more mild in the temperate region than it is in the tropical and boreal zones. Temperate forests account for 22 percent of Earth's forests. They are found in eastern North America, western and central Europe, and eastern Asia, among other places.

All woodland forests play an important role in the health of humans and the planet. Forests are home to the majority of Earth's plant and animal species. They provide people with goods such as food, timber, and medicine. Many people rely on forests for fuel and shelter.

More than One Name

The word *boreal* comes from the Latin word *borealis*, which means "northern wind." The boreal region is also sometimes referred to as *taiga*, a Russian word meaning "land of little sticks." In Canada the term boreal is often used to refer to southern forests, while taiga is used to refer to forests farther north.

CHAPTER TWO

CLIMATE AND WEATHER

Climate plays a big part in defining forest regions. Climate includes factors such as average temperature, amount of precipitation, and seasonal changes. An area's climate helps determine what plants and animals can live there.

Boreal Forests

Boreal forests are cold for most of the year. They have short summers and long winters. The average annual

Plants and animals in boreal forests must be able to survive cold winters.

Despite the cold, natural forest fires are common in boreal forests. They help the forests regenerate.

temperature across the boreal region is between a few degrees above freezing and 14 degrees Fahrenheit (-10°C).

The sun is never directly above the boreal region. It shines at an angle. As a result, its rays spread out over a larger area, making them less intense. This keeps the ground frozen nearly year-round. But in the short summer, the top layer thaws enough for plants to grow. Boreal trees tend to be small because it is hard for their roots to grow in the frozen ground. Average annual precipitation in boreal regions is between 15 and 40 inches (38–102 cm). Most comes in the form of snow.

Burning Boreal

Fire is important to boreal forests. It gets rid of old and diseased plants so that healthy plants can take their places. Unlike in other forests, most fires that occur in boreal forests start naturally. But fires are occurring more frequently today than in the past. One study found the rate of forest fires is higher than it has been in the past 10,000 years. And scientists are worried global warming may continue to make fires worse.

Temperate Forests

There are two kinds of temperate forests: deciduous and evergreen. Trees lose their leaves every year in deciduous forests. These forests exist in places where the four seasons are distinct but not extreme, such as

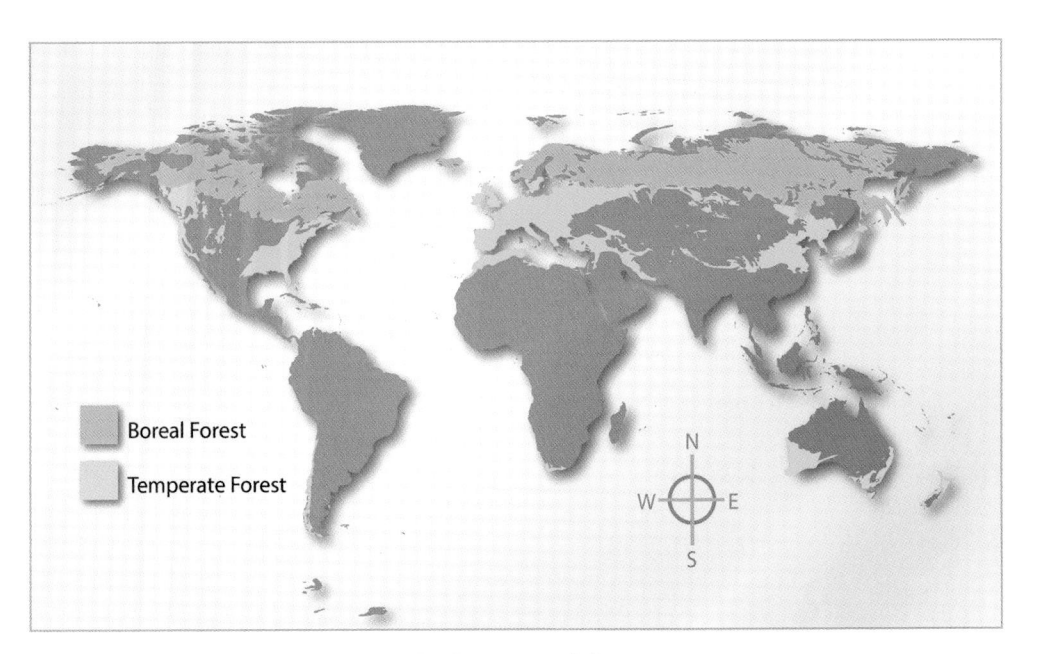

Woodlands around the World
This map shows the location of temperate and boreal forests on Earth. How does the map compare to what you have read in the text? How does it help you understand the types of places where different types of woodland forests grow?

the eastern half of North America, eastern Asia, and Western Europe. Summers tend to be warm. Winters often are frosty. Leaves on deciduous trees change to yellow, red, and orange before they fall. These forests receive between 30 and 60 inches (76–152 cm) of rain and snow per year.

Trees in evergreen temperate forests keep their leaves year-round. These forests have mild winters.

They receive a wide range of rainfall. But some are sandwiched between the ocean and a mountain range and receive a lot of rain. The Pacific Northwest of the United States and Canada is one example. The huge amounts of rain and mild temperatures in this part of the world provide a moist climate and long growing season. This stretch of woodland forest ecosystem is home to some of the world's oldest and largest trees.

Redwoods and Fog

California's Redwood National Park is home to the world's tallest tree. It rises 379 feet (116 m) above the forest floor. Its size is due to the unique Pacific Coast climate. In the warm summer months, fog is drawn inland off the ocean. It builds up over the redwoods. Then it slowly drips through the thick forest canopy, feeding the highest branches of the trees. This helps protect them from summer drought. Redwoods are found within 50 miles (80 km) of the coast, stretching from southern Oregon to central California. They can grow two to three feet (0.6–0.9 m) in one year.

CHAPTER THREE

WOODLAND FOREST PLANTS

Plants are producers in forests. This means they make their own food through a process called photosynthesis. Plants use their leaves to draw in energy from the sun and carbon dioxide from the air. They combine these with water to make sugar. Sugar helps plants grow. It also provides energy for other things in the ecosystem to grow.

Plants take in sunlight and turn it into food for forest animals.

Pine needles are shaped to protect the tree from the cold and retain water.

Plants of the Boreal Forest

Most trees in boreal forests are conifers, such as spruce, pine, and fir. These species have adapted to survive in the cold boreal biome. They have needles instead of leaves. The small, waxy surface of conifer needles helps the trees keep water and survive in the cold. Conifers have a pointed shape. This helps snow slide off the trees' branches instead of weighing them down.

Conifers tower over other boreal plants and form a thick canopy. The dark, moist environment below is perfect for moss and fungi. Approximately one third of the boreal forest floor is covered in moss. In old conifer forests, the entire forest floor is thick with moss.

A few types of deciduous trees, such as alder, birch, and aspen, have adapted to live in the boreal forest. These species have flexible branches that do not snap under the weight of snow. Some shrubs also grow well under the thick conifer cover. Blueberry, red osier dogwood, and honeysuckle are common.

Mushrooms

Mushrooms grow in many shapes, sizes, and varieties. They grow in both boreal and temperate forests and are an important part of the ecosystem. Mushrooms are decomposers. They feed off dead plant and animal matter. Many mushrooms and trees benefit from each other. The roots of the tree provide nutrients to the mushroom. In turn part of the mushroom attaches to the tree's roots and helps it gather nutrients. The top of the mushroom is aboveground. It helps the mushroom reproduce, like the fruit of a plant.

Red rhododendron bushes form a layer under the canopy and above the forest floor.

They make berries, which provide food for creatures of all sizes, including birds, squirrels, and bears.

Plants of the Temperate Forest

Temperate forests are made up mostly of either deciduous trees or evergreen trees. But many have a mix of both.

Deciduous forests have mainly broadleaved trees. These trees do not have needles. And most lose their leaves in fall. Tall trees, such as oak and maple, make up the top layer of deciduous forests. Shrubs grow in the middle layer. These include rhododendron, azalea, and mountain laurel. Ferns, short herbs, and wildflowers grow below the shrubs. In the spring, before new leaves have created a canopy, the forest floor is bright with sunlight. This allows many low-growing plants to produce fruit before late summer. The trees then produce nuts and seeds in the late summer and fall. This cycle helps ensure there is food for the forest animals when needed.

North America's Rain Forest

The temperate forests of North America's Pacific Northwest are unique. They are made up mainly of conifers instead of broadleaved trees. In this region, the winters are mild, only occasionally going below freezing. Most of the very heavy rain occurs in winter. Some of the world's biggest conifers, including redwood, Sitka spruce, yellow cedar, and western red cedar, are found here. Plants that grow on other plants are also common. The soil is rich with nutrients provided by fallen branches, needles, and leaves. This is the perfect environment for new plants to take root.

The Valdivian temperate rain forest in Chile gets vast amounts of rainfall and is in a warm climate. This allows broadleaved plants to keep their leaves year-round.

Some temperate forests get reliable rain throughout the year. In these places, the trees are broadleaved but do not lose their leaves. They are evergreens. In places where there is a lot of rain, temperate rain forests grow. These forests are found in southeast Australia, New Zealand, and southern South America. Trees in temperate rain forests often have waxy leaves that repel water.

Some temperate forests have long stretches without much rain. Sclerophyllous plants grow here. These broadleaved plants keep their leaves year-round. The leaves are small, hard, and thick. They help the plants hold onto water. The leaves often contain rich-smelling oils. This protects the plants by making them taste bad to animals. Eucalyptus trees are examples of sclerophyllous plants. They form a canopy so that other thick-leaved brush and grass can grow below.

EXPLORE ONLINE

This chapter discusses the plants of boreal forests, which is also known as taiga. How is the information given on the website below different from the information in this chapter? Which information is the same? How do the two sources present information differently? What can you learn from this website?

World Biomes: Taiga

mycorelibrary.com/woodland-forest-ecosystems

CHAPTER FOUR

WOODLAND FOREST ANIMALS

Forests are home to the majority of the world's animals. Mammals, birds, and insects have adapted to live in woodland forests. Some have thick fur to protect them from the cold winters. Others have big paws that make walking on the snow easier. Many creatures hibernate. Others migrate to follow food sources. Some birds avoid the cold by flying

The American marten has a thick coat of fur to keep it warm through harsh boreal winters.

south. But all of these animals depend on woodland forests to survive.

Animals of the Boreal Forest

Species of all sizes live in boreal forests. And each creature plays a special role in the ecosystem. Red squirrels, deer mice, and red-backed voles scurry across the ground. They are herbivores. This means they eat plants. To get ready for winter when food is hard to find, they store nuts and seeds.

Other herbivores have adapted to survive the harsh boreal winters. Caribou and elk migrate south in search of food. They travel farther than any other large animal in North America. The snowshoe hare has huge feet that help it stay on top of the snow. The animal also changes from a brown or gray color in the summer to white in the winter. This helps protect the hare from its main predator, the lynx.

The lynx is a carnivore. This means it eats meat. It depends on the snowshoe hare for food. The lynx has huge paws for chasing its prey across snow.

A snowshoe hare runs across the top of the snow to escape a predator.

Mountain lions, Siberian tigers, and wolves are carnivores of the boreal forest. These animals sit at the top of the food chain. They help control the populations of animals such as moose and caribou.

Brown bears are common in boreal forests. They are omnivores. This means they eat both plants and animals. They often snack on berries, nuts, and grasses or dig in the ground for roots. But bears also eat fish, rodents, foxes, and deer. They store fat in the spring and summer. Then they stay in their dens during the harsh winters.

Boreal Forest Food Web

Study this example of a boreal forest food web. The arrows show the flow of energy. How does the chart compare to what you have read in the text? In what ways does it help you understand the flow of energy in the forest?

The boreal forest has many types of birds. Most stay in the forest only for the summer breeding months. They then fly to warmer places as the weather turns cold. Birds are drawn to boreal forests in the summer because they have many wet areas to nest and are rich with insects to eat.

Temperate Forest Animals

Many animals that live in boreal forests also live in temperate forests. Some boreal animals have relatives that live in temperate forests. For example moose, wolverines, and brown bears are common in the boreal forest. And white-tailed deer, least weasels, and black bears are more common in temperate forests. These animals tend to be smaller.

Woodpeckers' Big Contribution

Woodpeckers play an important role in woodland forests. They peck holes into the trunks of trees to find food. They help control the population of many insects, including the spruce beetle. Woodpeckers also make bigger holes to nest and raise their young. But they never stay in one nest for long. When they abandon their nests, other birds take them over. Chickadees, wrens, and some types of owls use the empty nest holes.

Temperate weather also provides better conditions for cold-blooded animals to live in. Cold-blooded animals cannot control their own body temperature. They need to bask in the sun to stay warm. Snakes, salamanders, frogs, turtles, and newts live in temperate forests. But they must burrow into the ground or hibernate to survive the winter.

Insects are important in all forests. They help pollinate trees and provide food for many animals. They also help decompose dead material.

Frozen Alive to Survive

Some boreal forests in North America are home to wood frogs. Wood frogs have adapted to their climate in a unique way. When the cold winter months set in, the frogs hide inside logs or under leaves or rocks. During hibernation wood frogs' hearts stop beating. Ice crystals form in their blood. They even stop breathing. When the sun warms the air in spring, the frogs warm up and return to life.

In 2014 the government of British Columbia started decreasing the wolf population. They wanted to help caribou recover by getting rid of some of the animals' main predators. But scientist Paul Paquet argues getting rid of wolves does not address the underlying reason for the caribou decline:

> *Mountain and boreal caribou are clearly in trouble and on a long-term slide to extinction. . . . Habitat quality is the most important component of caribou recovery. It takes hundreds of years for a biomass of tree lichen to be adequate to sustain mountain caribou populations. . . . Extensive research has shown that the destruction of old forests and wilderness areas via industrial development has deprived caribou . . . and exposed them to levels of wolf predation they did not evolve with and are incapable of adapting to.*

Source: Paul Paquet. "Wolf and Caribou Management Backgrounder." Raincoast. Raincoast Conservation Foundation. February 7, 2015. Web. Accessed March 5, 2015.

What's the Big Idea?

Take a close look at this passage. What does Paquet say is the main cause of the caribou decline? What would be a better way to help the caribou, according to Paquet?

CHAPTER FIVE

PEOPLE AND WOODLAND FORESTS

People depend on forests for many reasons. Humans use trees to make items such as paper and boxes. They use wood as lumber for building and heating. Forests make oxygen people need. And forests help control global climates. Despite people's need for forests, they have destroyed huge areas of woodlands. This puts animal habitats and human well-being at risk.

Sawmills use big machines to turn trees into useable lumber.

Deforestation for agriculture breaks forests into smaller pieces.

Land-Use Change

The biggest reason humans cut down forests is for agriculture. Getting rid of forests allows more space for crops and grazing animals. One study reported that 70 percent of the cleared forests worldwide in the 1990s were changed into land for agriculture.

Sometimes forests are not cleared completely. Only parts are cut down for things like roads, mines, and dams. This can also be bad for forests. It breaks up areas of undisturbed woodlands. Roads can open areas up to logging or building. Roads also raise the risk of introducing invasive species to an area. All of these changes are kinds of deforestation. This means that they have a long-term effect on the forest.

Clear-cutting has a different effect on forests. Clear-cutting is when people cut down big parts of a forest to use the wood. Industries that make wood products often harvest trees by clear-cutting areas. The forests are then replanted, and new trees

Invasive Species

One way humans have hurt forests is by introducing nonnative plants, animals, and diseases. These are things that do not occur naturally in a certain place. Some nonnative plants and animals do not hurt forests. But many do. These are known as invasive species. They can harm the ecosystem in many different ways. For example, the emerald ash borer is a beetle that is not native to North America. It kills ash trees by eating through them. Invasive plants hurt forests in other ways. Common buckthorn, for instance, spreads quickly and competes for nutrients with native plants. It also does not allow sunlight to reach plants on the forest floor.

grow back slowly. But clear-cutting can have a big effect on forest ecosystems. For example, if trees near a river or stream are taken down, the water may not get enough shade. This can increase the water temperature and hurt plants and fish. Animals may also have a hard time finding food. This can push animals in search of food into places where humans live.

Climate Change

Forests play an important role in controlling the climate. Climate change is a result of too much carbon dioxide in the air. Carbon dioxide traps heat. This causes the planet to warm. Plants are able to take in carbon dioxide and release oxygen. But when trees are cut down or burned, they stop taking in carbon. They also release their stored carbon into the air. Approximately 1.6 billion tons (1.5 billion metric tons) of carbon dioxide are released into the atmosphere each year due to loss of forests.

Mining can put areas at risk of deforestation. In January 2005, the government of British Columbia introduced an online system that allowed anyone to claim an area for mining. The International Boreal Conservation Campaign said this in a report:

> *Under the B.C. Mineral Tenure Act, "free miners" may stake private land and then enter, use and occupy a mineral claim without notice to the surface landowner. . . . Notice must be given to property owners before exploration work commences, although only a single day's notice is required in Ontario. Disputes between prospectors and property owners are resolved by a commissioner, who can award compensation for damages caused to surface owners by exploration or mining development activities; however, the legislation is clear that mineral development is the priority use.*

> Source: "Mineral Exploration Conflicts in Canada's Boreal Forest." Boreal Canada. *International Boreal Conservation Campaign, May 2008. Web. Accessed March 5, 2015.*

Changing Minds

Imagine you are a landowner in British Columbia. Part of your land is boreal forest, and someone would like to explore it for mining. What would you say to the government in order to protect the forest? Include facts to support your argument.

ENTENTE SUR LA FORÊT BORÉALE CANADIENNE

Une entente historique pour une nouvelle
ère de collaboration en forêt boréale

THE CANADIAN BOREAL FOREST AGREEMENT

An Historic Agreement Signifying a New Era
of Joint Leadership in the Boreal Forest

THE FUTURE OF WOODLAND FORESTS

Climate change has helped bring attention to the importance of forests. When industries start new projects in forested areas, they are often met with large protests. But forest products help support many countries around the world. Slowly, industries, governments, and forest supporters are being forced to work together to protect forests and ensure economic and social well-being.

In 2010, leaders of Canada's major paper companies agreed to stop logging a huge area of boreal forest.

39

Sustainable Forestry

Forests cover approximately half of the area they once did. But in the late 1900s, people started paying more attention to the importance of forests. Loggers began cutting down trees in smaller, more spread-out sections. They waited longer for trees to develop before cutting down more trees. Today there are more standards for forestry. Companies can be certified to show they follow healthy forestry practices. This is good for their company and good for the forest.

Protecting the Forests

Well-managed forests could help reduce poverty, grow economies, and create a healthier environment. To help manage forests, the Program on Forests started in 1997. Its purpose is to take on issues such as economic development in poor nations, illegal logging, and climate change.

In 2000 the United Nations started the United Nations Forum on Forests (UNFF). The UNFF is made up of the United Nations members. Its main goal is to help manage and conserve forests.

The trend of deforestation is slowing. Approximately 32 million acres (13 million ha) of forests per year were lost between 2000 and 2010. But efforts to conserve and grow forests during those years made the net loss only 12.8 million acres (5.2 million ha) per year.

Like all ecosystems, forests are constantly adapting. But there is a limit to how much forests can change before they can no longer recover. Only time will tell if enough has been done to ensure the health of our forests in the future.

FURTHER EVIDENCE

Chapter Six covers the future of woodland forests and some of the efforts to save them. What is the main point of this chapter? What key evidence supports this point? Read the article at the website below. Does the information on the website support the main point of the chapter? What new evidence does it present?

National Geographic: Saving the Forests
mycorelibrary.com/woodland-forest-ecosystems

Great Smoky Mountain National Park

Approximately 80 percent of Great Smoky Mountain National Park is made up of deciduous forests. Covering the border of North Carolina and Tennessee, the park is home to more than 17,000 plant and animal species. Black bears are abundant, with approximately 1,500 bears living in the park.

Glen Finglas

Ancient woodlands in the United Kingdom are home to stands of trees that have existed in a natural state since before 1600. The largest ancient woodland in the United Kingdom is Glen Finglas, Scotland. It consists of 9,884 acres (4,000 ha) of forest.

Valdivian

The Valdivian broadleaved temperate rain forest in Chile and Argentina covers 96,000 square miles (248,000 sq km). It is the only temperate rain forest in South America. The Andes Mountains sit to the east of Valdivian. Its temperate forests are home to the world's smallest deer, the endangered pudu. And in humid areas, a species of bamboo grows in thick stands.

The white spirit bear found in the Great Bear Rain Forest is actually a rare type of black bear.

Great Bear Rain Forest

The 21-million-acre (8.5-million-ha) Great Bear Rain Forest stretches for 250 miles (402 km) on the mainland coast of British Columbia. It is part of the biggest coastal temperate rain forest on the planet. It is home to towering 1,000-year-old cedar trees and the rarely seen white spirit bear.

STOP AND THINK

Take a Stand

This book discusses deforestation and the impact it has on climate change. Do you think enough is being done to preserve our forests, or should more be done? Write a short essay explaining your opinion. Make sure to give reasons for your opinion, as well as facts and details to support those reasons.

Tell the Tale

This book opens with a brown bear hunting for salmon. Write 200 words telling the story of a brown bear's life in a woodland forest ecosystem. Describe the sights and sounds of the bear's environment. Where does the bear hunt? How far does it travel in a day? How does it spend its day? Be sure to set the scene, develop a sequence of events, and offer a conclusion.

Say What?

Studying ecosystems can mean learning a great deal of new vocabulary. Find five words in this book you have never heard before. Use a dictionary to find out what they mean. Then write the meanings in your own words, and use each word in a sentence.

Why Do I Care?

You might not live near a forest, but forests are likely still an important part of your life. How do forests affect your daily life? How might your life change if more forests are lost? How would your life be different if more forests were preserved?

GLOSSARY

agriculture
growing crops or raising animals to use for food and products

biome
a major global region mainly characterized by plant life and climate

broadleaved
having wide, flat leaves instead of needles

canopy
a ceiling of branches above the forest formed by the tallest trees

carbon dioxide
a gas that traps heat in the atmosphere

carcass
the dead body of an animal

conifer
an evergreen tree that does not lose its leaves in the winter

hibernate
to be in an inactive or dormant state during the cold winter months

nutrient
a substance that plants or animals need to live and grow

precipitation
water that falls to the ground as hail, mist, rain, sleet, or snow

taiga
another term for boreal forest, often used to refer to the more northern regions of the boreal forest

LEARN MORE

Books

Hurtig, Jennifer. *Deciduous Forests*. New York: AV2 by Weigl, 2012.

Miller-Schroeder, Patricia. *Boreal Forests*. New York: AV2 by Weigl, 2012.

Newland, Sonja. *Woodland and Forest Animals*. Mankato, MN: Riverstream Publishing, 2013.

Websites

To learn more about Ecosystems of the World, visit **booklinks.abdopublishing.com**. These links are routinely monitored and updated to provide the most current information available.

Visit **mycorelibrary.com** for free additional tools for teachers and students.

INDEX

ABOUT THE AUTHOR

Racquel Foran is a writer living in British Columbia, Canada. She has written a number of books for kids on subjects as varied as North Korea, organ transplants, and robotics. She enjoys helping kids develop a love for reading and learning.

31901059560658